the ephemeral nature ov

A.A.F.

Published by Arthur A. Filgueiras
Paperback ISBN 979-8-218-82950-6
Hardcover ISBN 979-8-218-83461-6

Cover and sigil design by A.A.F.

Illustration Credits:

All illustrations by Éliphas Lévi. Public Domain, sourced from the Internet Archive.

Images on pages 12 and 22 are from *The History of Magic* (1860).
Image on page 32 is from *Dogme et Rituel de la Haute Magie* (1856).

these poems are a testament to my ghost.

contents

introduction

Aleister Crowley was infamously known for saying

"Love is the law, love under will"

Most of us romanticize the idea of what love truly is, reducing its layers to a perversion of its true self. However, I believe that to understand love, we must choose it fully and with our whole selves.

When we think of someone we love so deeply that it aches, we feel how our heart opens in their presence, how we want to give, to protect, to hold them close. And we then notice, too, how close that love lives to fear, the fear of losing them, of not being enough, of being seen too clearly, and sometimes even to frustration or anger. But that doesn't mean the love is broken. It means it's real. Because love isn't clean or easy. It's not light without shadow.

The reality is, love and hate aren't opposites, they're bound together, born from the same intensity of care. When we try to divide them, to label one as good and the other as bad, but we forget that they often coexist. The more we try to control love, the more we turn it into something rigid, something small.

But love, when we let it be what it is, doesn't need to be perfect. It just needs to be chosen.

That's what it means to love under will, not to fall helplessly, but to decide, every day, to hold space for complexity. To meet another person not with expectations or possession, but with presence. To let them be who they are, and to offer your heart anyway.

Love isn't a feeling; it's a vow. A quiet rebellion against everything that tells us to guard ourselves.

And when it's real, it dissolves the lines between you and them. Not by force. But by tenderness, by trust, by the slow and steady courage of staying.

And so we choose those, not blindly, but with full awareness. With the fire of our will and the softness of our surrender. To walk beside them through every shadow and every light not as halves seeking to be whole, but as sacred opposites moving together toward the place where all division ends.

We give ourselves to a union not to be completed, but to be consumed.

As they are the mirror we step through, the flame we walk into, the vow we speak not just with words, but with the whole of who we are.

We will choose those, again and again, until there is nothing left of ourselves but of each other...

love is the law.

love under will.

Liber I:

the Mirror

?!

in seams
do I remain,

or
merely remain?

painted skin.
who are you?

yes, hello?
yes, hello.

who, am i?
i am what you show.

yes, hello?
yes, hello.

mirrored reflections.
ov another.
ov another.

another...
incomplete.

stained mirror
wiped clean.
still stained.

my shadow.
mocks me.
unknowingly.

it mocks itself.

pane
fragmenting
revealed
eyes closed.

in my reflection
i speak.
no sound.

who is talking back?

Liber II:

the Ghost

see me
with your silent voice
hear me
with your empty eyes

no one present

ode to genesis

where are you going?
i'm traveling

could you stay?
i'm just traveling

are you returning?
i'll be traveling

where are you going?
i'm traveling

paralyzed
i am traveling
into emptiness
brighter than light

where are *you*?

clothed in woe
naked.
without goodbyes

dreamscapes
wandering through
lament gardens
blossomed in decay
consumed by rot
desolate leaves
left behind
...fragments ov perception

i awake
into *grief*

two mouths
one breath
lungs filled
both empty

the hunger
borrows the core
hallows the flesh

left only
unfulfilled
wondering
wandering

onto the next.
into the next.

fleshes worn
for us
for them

both truths,
both lies,
neither shown

Liber III:

the Will

abyss.
punishment.
birthed
ov *absence*...

deaf
to screams ov *nothing*,
beneath the eclipse
ov a hallowing husk.

left
within the *never*

echoing silence,
echoing silence,
silence

louder than love

shall the *never*
devour
what remains?

noises
inside
outside

noises
awake
dreaming

noises
in silence

noises
in noises

noises.
never ending

each drag

thoughts inhaled
nothing exhaled

one more.
carton is empty.

a spider
molts itself,

one left hollowed.
one left alone.

infinite waves,
binding currents

awaits *my* calling,
a horizon

horizonless sea
i stand
drifting forever

beside me
a buried branch

sitting
far away.

brightest moonlight
never enough
to lighten

inverted.
i orgasm.

coagulated.
decay conceived.

consuming itself
the snake
eternally defecating

thousands ov eyes
cloaked in shadows
bound by whispers

crackling
ov ashes
flowing in a river

first day ov *dying*
december 3, 1986
i screamed life
into a breath

?

love without law.

love without will.

the ephemeral nature ov

A.A.F.

all words were solely human written

www.ingramcontent.com/pod-product-compliance
Lightning Source LLC
LaVergne TN
LVHW041204080426
835511LV00006B/738